THE CURE FOR THE CHRISTMAS CRAZIES

WestBow Press books may be ordered through booksellers or by contacting:

WestBow Press
A Division of Thomas Nelson & Zondervan
1663 Liberty Drive
Bloomington, IN 47403
www.westbowpress.com
1 (866) 928-1240

Because of the dynamic nature of the Internet, any web addresses or links contained in this book may have changed since publication and may no longer be valid. The views expressed in this work are solely those of the author and do not necessarily reflect the views of the publisher, and the publisher hereby disclaims any responsibility for them.

ISBN: 978-1-5127-0797-7 (sc)
ISBN: 978-1-5127-0798-4 (e)

Library of Congress Control Number: 2015913015

Printed in the United States of America.

WestBow Press rev. date: 09/28/2015

This is a work of fiction. All of the characters, names, incidents, organizations, and dialogue in this novel are either the products of the author's imagination or are used fictitiously.

WESTBOW
PRESS®
A DIVISION OF THOMAS NELSON
& ZONDERVAN

THE CURE FOR THE CHRISTMAS CRAZIES

Written and Illustrated by

April Hartmann

Who is Santa Claus?

Have you ever wondered how Santa Claus got started?
The answer may surprise you. Long ago, in the fourth century,
lived a man named Nicholas. Nicholas spent his life serving God
and helping people. As a bishop, he loved to teach others about
Jesus. He gave generously to the poor, protected children, and is
said to have performed many miracles.
Now he is known as Saint Nicholas.

Saint Nicholas is
celebrated all over the world.
In the country of Holland, children leave shoes outside their
doors, hoping to receive a treat from "Sinter Klaas." In the
United States, children hang stockings on Christmas Eve,
eager for Santa Claus to fill them with gifts.

Do you think that Santa Claus still keeps Jesus in his heart?
Of course he does! In the story of the Christmas Crazies,
Santa Claus helps our friend Norbert the elf teach others
about Jesus.

with love and thanks to Steve –
for supporting my crazy ideas.

November 1st

Dear Santa,
I know you get lots of letters asking for toys,
but I need your **help!**

My name is Norbert Jinglejensen. I'm 8 years
old, and I live on Snowflake Lane here in the
North Pole. My dad, Milo Jinglejensen,
makes bikes at the workshop.

Something crazy is
going on in my
neighborhood and
I just don't get it...

It's the day right after Halloween and my neighbor, Mr. Sparklekowski, already put up a bunch of Christmas lights. Decorations are popping up all over our neighborhood! It won't be Jesus' birthday for 55 more days. Why is everyone decorating so early? Should my family put up lights too?

Your Friend,
Norbert Jinglejensen

November 7th

Dear Norbert,

Goodness! It sounds like your neighbors are very excited about Christmas coming. Your family can put up lights whenever they are ready. There's no need to rush.

Just remember, the reason we decorate with lights is because God sent Jesus to light up the whole world. At the workshop, we deck the halls for Christmas all year long. It reminds us to let God's love shine in our hearts as we build toys for children.

Decorating is fun. But don't forget that Christmas is truly about the birth of Jesus. Otherwise, you could catch the Christmas Crazies. You can be my big helper by reporting back with news of any more craziness.

Love,
Santa

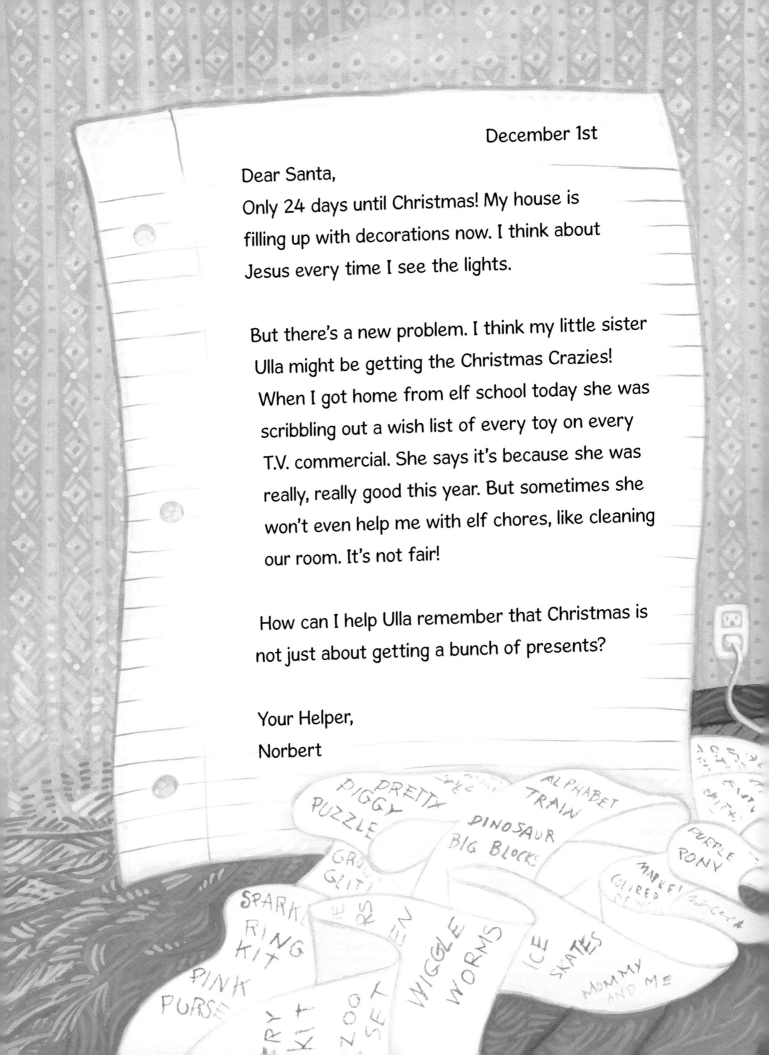

December 1st

Dear Santa,
Only 24 days until Christmas! My house is
filling up with decorations now. I think about
Jesus every time I see the lights.

But there's a new problem. I think my little sister
Ulla might be getting the Christmas Crazies!
When I got home from elf school today she was
scribbling out a wish list of every toy on every
T.V. commercial. She says it's because she was
really, really good this year. But sometimes she
won't even help me with elf chores, like cleaning
our room. It's not fair!

How can I help Ulla remember that Christmas is
not just about getting a bunch of presents?

Your Helper,
Norbert

December 5th

Dear Norbert,

Jumpin' Jinglebells! Ulla's very long wish list just arrived. It's true—her behavior hasn't been perfect. But it's not easy for anyone to be good all year long. So God teaches us to have a forgiving heart.

Here is a story that might help Ulla think differently about her wish list. When Jesus was born, a bright twinkling star rose in the sky. Three wise men followed the star from far away. When they found little Jesus they were filled with joy and wanted to honor him. They had only three gifts for him—gold, frankincense, and myrrh—but those gifts were very important treasures.

My favorite part of Christmas is giving. When we give gifts to others, we are sharing God's love. Perhaps you could talk to Ulla about honoring Jesus with a gift this Christmas. One of the best gifts children can offer is being kind and helpful to others.

Love,
Santa

December 9th

Dear Santa,

Big news! I told Ulla about the three wise men and now she sees how giving can honor Jesus and bring joy to others. By giving gifts of kindness, we can share God's love too. We both cleaned our whole room together and helped our mom set up the nativity scene.

Now Ulla just wants "good-smelling hot dogs" for Christmas, you know, "frank and scents!" I told her that frankincense is not food. Really it's some stuff that smells nice when you burn it, kind of like a candle. She still thinks Jesus would have liked hot dogs better!

I'll tell you if I see anymore signs of the Christmas Crazies.

Your Helper,
Norbert

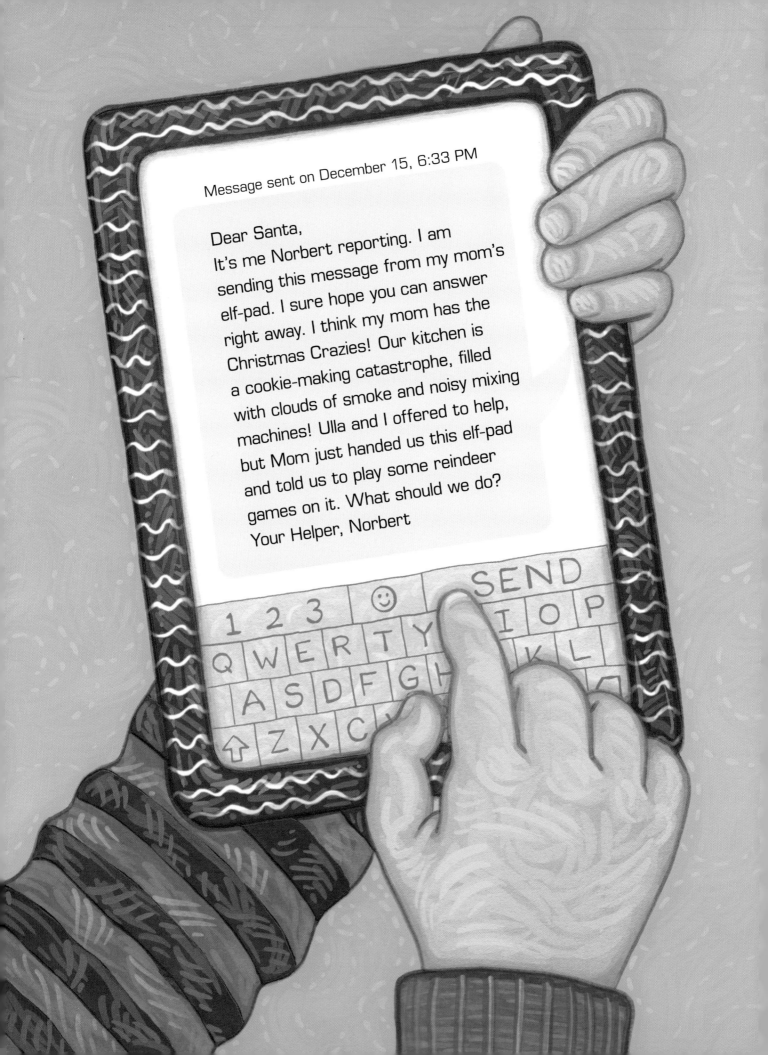

Message sent on December 15, 6:33 PM

Dear Santa,
It's me Norbert reporting. I am sending this message from my mom's elf-pad. I sure hope you can answer right away. I think my mom has the Christmas Crazies! Our kitchen is a cookie-making catastrophe, filled with clouds of smoke and noisy mixing machines! Ulla and I offered to help, but Mom just handed us this elf-pad and told us to play some reindeer games on it. What should we do?
Your Helper, Norbert

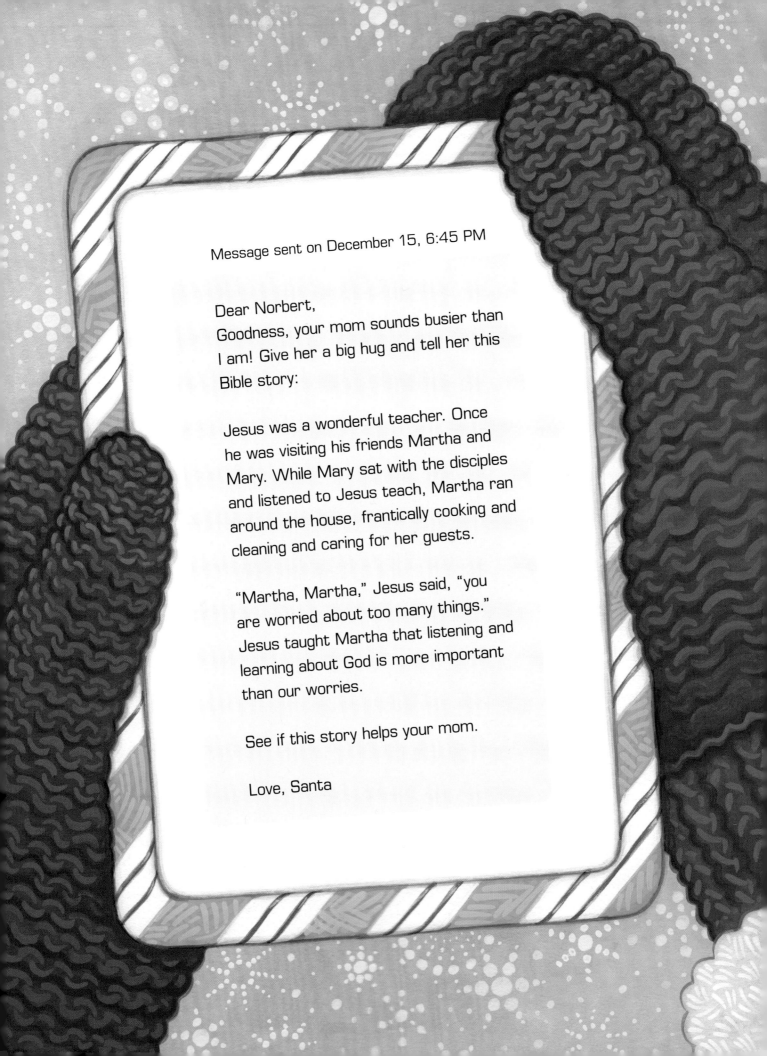

Message sent on December 15, 6:45 PM

Dear Norbert,
Goodness, your mom sounds busier than I am! Give her a big hug and tell her this Bible story:

Jesus was a wonderful teacher. Once he was visiting his friends Martha and Mary. While Mary sat with the disciples and listened to Jesus teach, Martha ran around the house, frantically cooking and cleaning and caring for her guests.

"Martha, Martha," Jesus said, "you are worried about too many things." Jesus taught Martha that listening and learning about God is more important than our worries.

See if this story helps your mom.

Love, Santa

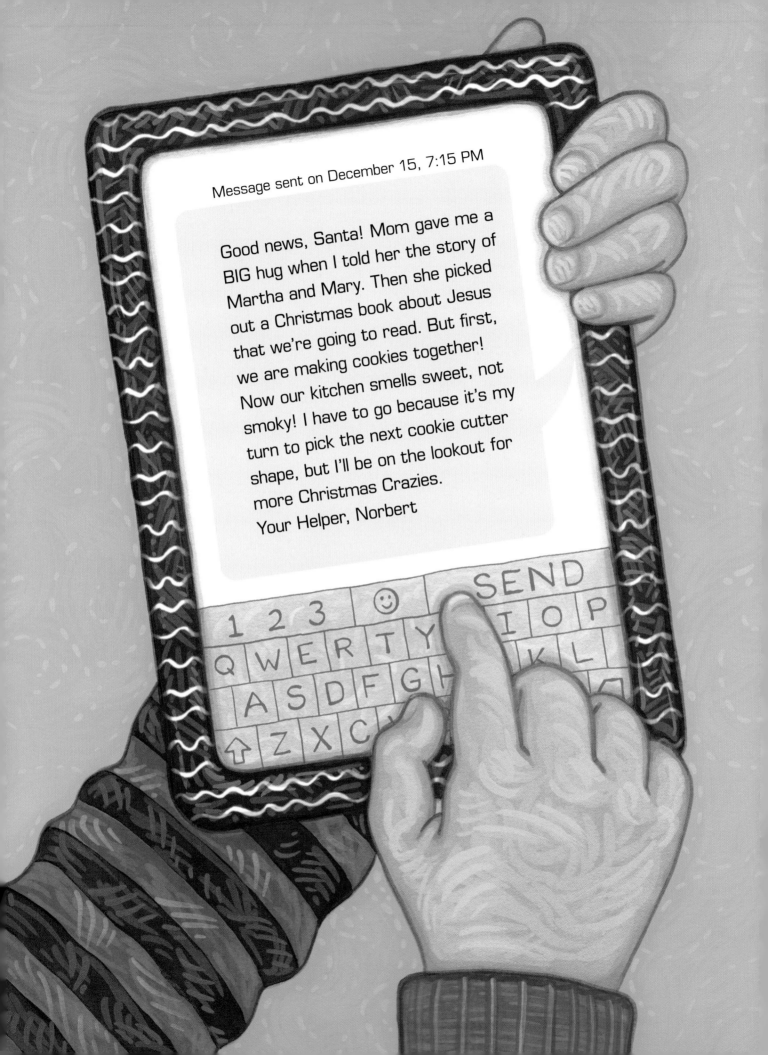

December 23rd

Dear Santa,
Breaking news! I think my dad has the Christmas Crazies now! My family wanted to take a sleigh ride to check out all the pretty decorations, but Dad has just been dashing from store to store. He's buying all kinds of presents for our family. I know that giving is more important than getting, but this much giving seems crazy! You are probably super busy loading up your sleigh, but I sure hope you can help again. What should we do?

Your Helper,
Norbert

Merry Christmas Norbert!

You have been such a good little elf this year. Your dad loves you very much, and it makes him happy to give you presents. Make sure you say, "Thank you!"

Thank you, Dad!

God also loves you very much and gives you many gifts, but they don't come from a store. God gave you a loving family, jolly friends and a beautiful world filled with many wonders to enjoy. But the greatest gift of all is when God sent Jesus on Christmas Day. Jesus taught us to love one another and to love God. You remember what to say when you receive a gift, right? Maybe you can help your dad remember these things by giving him a gift. But instead of buying something from a store, give him a gift from your heart.

Love, Santa

Merry Christmas, Dad!

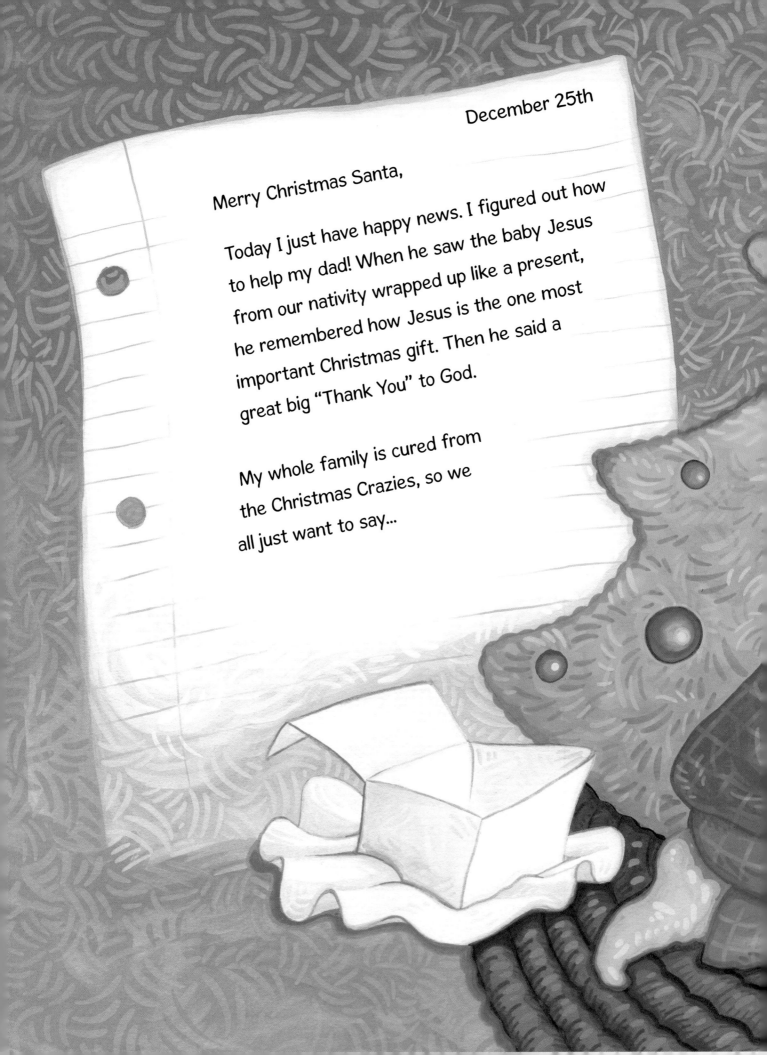

December 25th

Merry Christmas Santa,

Today I just have happy news. I figured out how to help my dad! When he saw the baby Jesus from our nativity wrapped up like a present, he remembered how Jesus is the one most important Christmas gift. Then he said a great big "Thank You" to God.

My whole family is cured from the Christmas Crazies, so we all just want to say...

Thank you, Santa!

You can learn even more about these Bible stories!

Jesus is the light of the world: John 8:12, John 12:36
The Magi (three wise men) Visit the Messiah: Matthew 2: 1-12
At the Home of Martha and Mary: Luke 10:38-42
The Birth of Jesus: Matthew 1: 18-23, Luke 2: 1-13

About the Author

April Hartmann's inspiration to write
began back in art school, admiring the
playful dance between pictures and words
found in children's books. Her respect for
this craft grew stronger while studying
the books her own children loved. After
years of illustrating for religious publishers,
and a passionate deepening of faith, that little
writing spark became a burning flame.

Today she has more than twenty years of experience as a professional
illustrator and is a member of the Society of Children's Book Writers and
Illustrators. A wife and mother of 3, April Hartmann is enjoying life in the
hills of western Pennsylvania. When she's not painting or writing, she's
usually chauffeuring to soccer and gymnastics practices. She also enjoys
volunteering at the elementary school and teaching religious education
at her local parish.

See more of April Hartmann's artwork at:

ahcreations.com